T1D Mindset Reset

21 Days to an Intentional Relationship with Type 1 Diabetes

By Dr. Hannah Hamlin, DO, T1D

Contents

Today is the day. Today is the day you are making big strides forward in your diabetes care. You bought this program, you decided you wanted to put energy into your mindset about diabetes and that DECISION is honorable. Today you voluntarily took the way you think about diabetes into your own hands. By committing to a book like this a part of you has acknowledged that your thoughts about diabetes are something that you have the choice to learn to impact through your knowledge and thoughts. Part of you said, I have control in influencing the way I think and the beauty in that is huge.

Before we get started, let's talk about the intention of this program. The intention is to evaluate your thoughts and feelings related to diabetes and to determine if they are holding you back or helping you to be your best self.

This content teaches you ways of doing things that may be different than your current patterns. I believe understanding the wide gradient of ways to look at situations better allows us to pick where we would like our own perspectives to lay. The thoughts and statements this book presents are examples that you could choose to incorporate into your thoughts about diabetes. I challenge you to consider them, try them out for a while and notice if they help you to see things in a new way.

I also challenge you to create your own list of thoughts you want to believe about diabetes and its effects on you. I truly believe that this has the potential to completely change your relationship with type 1 diabetes. I have seen it be a game changer for happiness with diabetes in myself, in my friends and in my patients. This book was written from a place of love and wanting to share all the good that diabetes has brought to my life.

Gratitude: I have had an incredible amount of support from family, friends and physicians growing up that have helped lead me to the insights in this book. I am immensely grateful for all of the support and love I have received. I would also like to thank everyone involved with Texas Lions Camp for giving me a community to call home.

Disclaimer: This book details the author's personal experiences with and opinions about type 1 diabetes and mindset. The author is not your healthcare provider. The author and publisher are providing this book and its contents on an "as is" basis and make no representations or warranties of any kind with respect to this book or its contents. The author disclaims all such representations and warranties, including for example warranties of merchantability and healthcare for a particular purpose. In addition, the author and publisher do not represent or warrant that the information accessible via this book is accurate, complete or current. The statements made about products and services have not been evaluated by the U.S. Food and Drug Administration. They are not intended to diagnose, treat, cure, or prevent any condition or disease. **Please consult with your own physician or healthcare specialist regarding the suggestions and recommendations made in this book.** Except as specifically stated in this book, neither the author or publisher, nor any authors, contributors, or other representatives will be liable for damages arising out of or in connection with the use of this book. This is a comprehensive limitation of liability that applies to all damages of any kind, including (without limitation) compensatory; direct, indirect or consequential damages; loss of data, income or profit; loss of or damage to property and claims of third parties. **You understand that this book is not intended as a substitute for consultation with a licensed healthcare practitioner, such as your physician**. Before you begin any healthcare program, or change your lifestyle in any way, you will consult your physician or another licensed healthcare practitioner to ensure that you are in good health and that the examples contained in this book will not harm you. This book provides content related to physical and/or mental health issues. As such, use of this book implies your acceptance of this disclaimer. The Content is not intended to be a substitute for professional medical advice, diagnosis, or treatment. Always seek the advice of your **physician** or other qualified health provider with any questions you may have regarding a medical condition. If you are or become suicidal or homicidal, please contact your local **emergency medical services**.

MICROCHAPTER 1: You are not your disease.

You are not your disease. You are not diabetes. Diabetes is a part of you, it is not you. It is easy to get consumed in the daily routine and mind chatter of diabetes and blood glucose control. It is easy to let it become overwhelming. It is easy to slip into an intense identity perspective and let diabetes consume the other things that you are. I let this happen to me for a few years. Finding myself after realizing this was a huge gift.

Regardless of how many times you've been called or heard the word 'diabetic', know that you are a PERSON with diabetes. You do person things, you have person goals, and person responsibilities. You are a person first. This may seem obvious to some of you, this may be a reminder to others. The reminder of who you are and who you were before diagnosis can only serve as an asset as we begin this positive change. Remind yourself of who you really are behind the chronic daily happenings of diabetes.

Take Inventory of you.

- Take inventory of the things that you are. Write them below, as many as you can think of - examples include: human, artist, student, lover of movies, author, sister, brother, store clerk, painter, space x enthusiast, women, man, daughter, son, mother, father, teacher, skate border, social drinker, monopoly winner, boy/girlfriend.

- Set a timer for 3 minutes and spend it specifically thinking of how diabetes has affected these things about you, if at all. Write out one sentence summarizing your conclusion of this exercise.
-
- Write out 3 things you would really want to be if you had no limitations. Explain why for each number listed below, the **why** is the most important part. Take your time on this. It can take awhile to get our imagination going. Ex: dancer, doctor, mother, runner, world traveler, YouTuber, etc.
- 1. because
-
-
- 2. because
-
-
- 3. because
-

Re-read your answer to the previous questions. Are you holding yourself back? If so, did you realize it? How often are we honest with ourselves about the things that we subconsciously let diabetes hold us back from? Circle the number/s of the questions above that you feel diabetes has distanced you from dreaming about. If you circled more than one ask yourself which one bothers you the most or stirs up the most emotional reaction. Then answer the question below based on it.

- Am I really unable to do this with type 1 diabetes or does type 1 diabetes just make it harder/more challenging/slower/different?
    - Highlight one: Impossible ○/More challenging ○/No effect ○
- Would the benefit of fulfilling this role be worth experiencing the extra difficulty diabetes places on it?
    - Highlight one: Worth it ○/Too tough ○/I'd need to look into more ways to make it happen before I decide ○.

- Is there someone who has already done it or would have insight on it that you could reach out to?
    - Highlight one: Yes ○/No ○

- If yes, who is it?

- If not, try googling it!

This exercise is allowing us to pinpoint our limiting beliefs around becoming our best selves while living with type 1 diabetes. This helps us call out anything that we have been subconsciously avoiding due to diabetes. This is an important place to start as it helps us understand ways in which we may most want to change our thoughts and beliefs about how diabetes affects our current and future lives.

Here is a personal example:

Uncomfortable thought: I'm not smart or healthy enough to handle the stress of medical school. What if I have to sacrifice my health or my grades if there is too much on my plate at once? It might not be a good idea for me.

Limiting belief: It would be too hard to take care of my own health and learn to help others with theirs.

Underlying Emotion: Fear of letting diabetes overwhelm me. Fear of not being able to go to medical school because I have diabetes.

Shift in thinking: Medical school with diabetes knowledge would help me understand some of what's taught about glucose control and my diabetes experience will help me understand what it's like to be a patient. Maybe diabetes would help me be an even better doctor than I would have been without it.

All beliefs could have become true if I had let them. I chose the thought that felt best to me and decided to go with it. This is so simple. It's an easy example of a perspective shift that was empowering and ultimately changed the course of my career.

We get to pick the story we tell ourselves.

In the end, I went to medical school and the last two years of school I lowered my HbA1c to 5.5%, the best of my life thus far.

"You are not your disease. You are not diabetes. Diabetes is a part of you, it is not who you are".

MICROCHAPTER 2: You are not broken.

"Broken crayons still color." This goofy quote I read at one point growing up and somehow felt emotionally understood by it. My internal thoughts went like this, 'I was doing what most other humans do to function even though I was broken. Parts of me just didn't work and I had to make up for their slack and do all these extra tasks just to function." I used every diabetes action in my life as a reminder that something was 'wrong' with me. This did not feel good. My personal conclusion at that time was that I WAS BROKEN. This was a major issue that was affecting my overall quality of life in a big way. I felt broken for years after my diagnosis and didn't truly realize that was a recurrent thought in my mind for a long time. I certainly didn't realize the impact that it had on my self-worth, my self-love and my self-belief. Retrospectively, I think I let these thought patterns hold me back from a lot of cool experiences.

My perspective in the example above left me feeling that each time I 'had' to do something to take care of my diabetes I was 'fixing' my brokenness. I was making up for my inefficiencies. That didn't feel good. Once I changed this internal dialog to appreciating the healthy body I do have, I was able to start seeing my daily diabetes tasks as a way to show love to my body, not as fixing my brokenness. This felt so much lighter and empowering.

Opportunity to try this thought on: As a patient, physician, and scientist it is my personal and medical opinion that if you have diabetes YOU ARE NOT BROKEN. You may be different than others around you. You may need extra things to get through the day than your family. You may need more snacks/testing breaks than your peers. This makes you different. Not broken.

A way I like to explain this to my friends is that type 1 diabetes is like running your metabolism in manual while everyone else is driving automatic. We have to change gears more often and use both feet. It's a little more complicated to be healthy, but once you learn how, you can function metabolically just as well as everyone else. We don't have a broken engine. We have a different model.

You can always make a shift in thought. I am unworthy to have as much fun out dancing with friends because my blood sugar is running higher than usual vs. I think dancing may help relieve the stress that's causing my blood sugar to run higher. I am unable to give back as much at the fundraiser because I had to stop and test my blood sugar and treat a low vs. I love being able to take care of myself, my disease, and help a good cause.

You may already know this. You may already have passed this phase, or maybe you never fell into this line of thinking. That's wonderful! I personally would have benefited from hearing someone say that I wasn't broken. I needed someone to lay it out simply, that I was whole. You can have diabetes and be whole. A whole beautiful, strong capable human. You have everything that you need within you to create a happy, healthy, and fulfilling life.

Ask yourself this honestly: DO I FEEL BROKEN because of diabetes? Do I feel less than? Have I ever felt this way? If so type/write out the questions below:

- How do I feel broken?

- Why exactly do I feel broken?

- Is this actually true?

- Am I attached to the victim mindset (this is a hard one)? If so, how?

- How do I ultimately want to feel about this?

Do it. Decide right now that this is how you want to feel and who you want to be. You can choose to dwell on the things that are harder, more time consuming, more tedious, or you can choose to dwell on all the things you can do. If you don't want to feel broken and you feel you don't have to anymore then say out loud, "I am not broken". Say it to yourself. Find a mirror, put your phone in selfie mode if you have to, look yourself in the eye and decide. Affirm it. Right now, audibly, before you keep reading. "I am not broken". Let it go. Tell yourself you're ready to move on from this feeling that isn't serving you.

"I am not broken, I am whole."

There is a chance that you may not have spoken to yourself in the mirror before, in which case it will probably feel pretty weird. That's okay, let it feel weird. Self-growth takes us out of our comfort zone. Saying things out loud to an empty room isn't for the faint of heart. It may feel awkward, or silly, or super weird but there is a reason. When we say things out loud the words, we affirm travel through more neurons in our brain than if they were just a passing thought or something that we read. It will be more impactful in your neurochemistry this way and help you create a new thought pattern faster. Remember, you have diabetes after all, by default you're already pretty freaking strong.

What if it really makes a difference? What if it doesn't? Is being slightly uncomfortable for 3 seconds worth the benefit it may have? It's up to you.

You may need to repeat it. You may need to say it every day for a while before it fully sinks in. It's a decision you can make in the now, you don't need to research it, think about it, read blogs about it. You just need to decide in your own mind, that you don't want to feel broken and you don't need to anymore.

Perspective is everything.
Beta cells are the cells that make insulin in our body. The cells that don't work in people with type 1 diabetes.
Beta cells are approximately 50% of the islet cells in the pancreas.
Islet cells are approximately 1-2% of pancreatic volume.
The pancreas is one organ.

There are approx. 79 organs in the human body (this number varies greatly among which anatomy textbook you read but you get the gist).
Therefore, people with type 1 diabetes have 78.9 functioning organs making up their body.
That's approximately 99.87% of your body's organs that work!

"99.87% beautifully working physiology. #gratitude"

If that was a grade it would be an A+, if it was a research study it would be statistically significant, if it was the majority of things on this planet it would round up to 100%.

*I realize these stats seem to belittle the amount of effort it takes to make up for that <0.2% in our daily lives, but it provides a unique perspective of the bigger picture.

If feelings of being broken come back remember, it's just a few cells in one organ. Less than one percent is not enough to physically hold you back from accomplishing your dreams, from becoming who you want to be, from loving the world or from loving yourself.

MICROCHAPTER 3: Your thoughts about diabetes impact your actions.

Picture a morning when you wake up late, your blood sugar is higher than expected, you show up rushed to wherever you're going and then realize you forgot some important part of your diabetes kit. I feel like some version of this story is identifiable to all of us. If your thoughts are coming from a place of hating that you have diabetes the fault of the rough morning will likely be placed on diabetes. If you are coming from a place of diabetes being neutral or positive in your life you will be more likely to blame the rough morning on being human. You could have forgotten your keys; it didn't have to be your insulin. This difference is impactful. This difference can impact how you feel.

Opportunity to try this thought on: If you are mad at diabetes, you are more likely to find reasons to make you more mad at it. We actually have some cool scientific understanding of this phenomenon, if you're interested in nerding out, you can look up the reticular activating system (RAS).

If every time your blood sugar is high you blame yourself with thoughts like, "I should have done XYZ" or "it's not my fault diabetes is too hard" the event is likely to feel unfavorable and unpleasant. Only blaming yourself like in the first example isn't favorable because there are more things that can control our blood sugar than we can always control. For example, hormones or hidden sugars are ridiculously unpredictable. Only blaming your circumstances and not taking any credit for the high blood sugar isn't favorable either because if we believe we truly have no control we will not find reason to make choices that result in a better outcome next time. These two examples are on opposite ends of the spectrum. A healthy mindset, in my opinion, is found somewhere in between.

As humans, we are designed to avoid unpleasant things, this is a survival mechanism. Once we burn our hand on the stove, we are likely to be more careful to avoid touching the stove again to protect ourselves. This concept applies to thoughts too, if every time we see a high blood sugar number we instinctively create self-blame or fall into a victim mindset allowing ourselves to feel sad, angry, helpless, etc. This may deter us from wanting to test our blood sugar next time we feel high and thus we may put off correcting our blood sugar. This example shows how our thoughts about diabetes can impact our actions. This may not be where you are right now, but I do believe it is a common phase of diabetes burnout. Chronic negative emotions are not consistent with vitality and we are likely to subconsciously avoid them, thus avoiding their triggers. Understanding this phenomenon in human psychology is very helpful in understanding why we do things.

It goes both ways, you are excited about your new long acting dose change because you think you're going to have hypoglycemia less frequently and therefore you test more frequently to check to see if it's working, thus you catch more lows before they become severe. Your positive anticipatory attitude helps you with a better outcome as well as the change in insulin dosing. Therefore, your thoughts created an even more favorable result.

Can you think of three examples over the past week that show how your thoughts about diabetes may have led to a specific blood sugar outcome:

1.

2.

3.

You may have already learned from experience that getting mad at yourself for having high or low blood sugar levels doesn't actually stop them from becoming high or low again. Let this sink in. Decide if this is something you want to keep doing if you are already doing it.

I recommend choosing the pep-talk format to replace this form of thinking. When our blood sugar is out of whack, we deserve more love, not less. Think about what you would say to a younger sibling, child, best friend in this position.

"Hey, you got this. It's okay that it didn't work out this time. We're always learning. What can we learn from this to help prevent it from happening again"?

Next time I have a diabetes outcome I don't like, instead of getting upset with myself. I will choose to say:

Pro Tip: Write this new thought on a post it note and put it next to your blood sugar meter or type it somewhere in your phone if you use a phone based CGM (continuous glucose monitor).

MICROCHAPTER 4: It's not your fault.

Chances are blame and guilt are not serving you. The examples in the previous chapter explain this well. Let's dive a little deeper into understanding the impact of this in our own lives.

It's not your or anyone else's fault. Truth is there's a lot we still don't know about diabetes from a medical standpoint. We know how it happens but we don't always know why. What we do know is that there are many many many factors that create an impact that can cause it in a person. It takes the perfect combination of our genes being susceptible and our environment providing a trigger for our immune systems to get confused and mount an attack on our beta cells. #epigenetics

Can you identify unnecessary guilt that you are carrying around? Yes ○ /No ○
Are you blaming yourself or anyone else? Yes ○ /No ○ /Both ○
If so, whom?

If so, really consider if the self-punishment and negative emotions that guilt or blame are really serving you. Do they bring any benefit to your life? Yes○/No○
If you could drop them completely, would you? Yes ○ /No ○
Do you feel empowered enough to drop them?Yes ○ /No ○

This may be another thought to let go. Say aloud, "Diabetes is not my fault" or "Diabetes is not their fault" or "Diabetes is no-one's fault". Use the mirror. Look yourself in the eye. Let it go. You can do this.

If you don't feel empowered to let go of guilt, it's likely that you are either not ready or just don't know how. Both are okay. If you don't know how to and you would like to, the answer lies in convincing yourself otherwise. Convincing yourself that.... diabetes is a gift. It's here to teach you something. Make you stronger, smarter, braver. It's here to help motivate you to make your wildest dreams come true.

It's not how my life is going; it's how I'm choosing to see it. It's the story I'm telling myself every day, all day of how things 'are'. It took me sitting down and re-writing my whole life story outside of a 'feeling sorry for myself' mindset. It took me imagining the best version of myself and how I would want to feel about life.

How would the best version of you see your story?

MICROCHAPTER 5: Victim or Hero? It is your choice.

It's easy to think life isn't fair with diabetes. It's easy to assume diabetes makes things harder in your life. It's easy to say, 'woe is me." A victim mindset can be explained very simply in the words, thoughts and feelings that align with, " I feel sorry for myself." I've been there. You might have been there. Once I realized I was blaming diabetes for things it had nothing to do with in my life, I was able to decide that I didn't want to do that anymore. I realized I was using diabetes as an excuse not to be my best self.

We can so desperately want other people to know that this was not our fault, that diabetes totally sucks some days and that we are trying the best we can but sometimes we are learning through failure because blood sugar can have a tendency to be unpredictable at times. It's easy to almost want to be in the victim role just to offset the bystanders that may try to blame all this extra responsibility on us. This is real. It's raw. It's probably uncomfortable to read. It's definitely uncomfortable to write. I think this kind of thing takes honesty and bravery to even think about.

Truth is, you can choose to be the victim or the hero of your own life with type 1 diabetes. You choose this every day, multiple times a day, with every thought you have in the direction of diabetes. It really only takes recognizing which role you're playing and consciously deciding if you are the victim or the hero.

Like any habit, it takes practice and repetition. It is possible to grow in this area of your life. You are capable of being a hero. You really already are, you just have to realize it and own it if you haven't already. You save your life from diabetes every single day. You do things every single day that most of the population can't even imagine doing. You do hard things so you can give love, make a positive impact, help others, live the full human experience. You are your own hero every day and you will be the rest of your life. You are the hero to all the people you positively impact in your life every single day. You are enough. The only thing that can truly make you a victim in your own head is your own thoughts. Choose accordingly.

Opportunity to try this thought on: I can't eat that because I have diabetes. Woe is me vs. I am choosing not to eat that because it doesn't make me feel good. I am empowered to make healthy choices as a human.

Identify five recurring thoughts about diabetes that you have monthly/weekly/daily that leave you with uncomfortable feelings. Try to flip the place this thought is coming from to a place of empowerment.

Uncomfortable thought:

New empowering thought:

Uncomfortable thought:

New empowering thought:

Uncomfortable thought:

New empowering thought:

Uncomfortable thought:

New empowering thought:

Uncomfortable thought:

New empowering thought:

"Feeling sorry for yourself, and your present condition is not only a waste of energy but the worst habit you could possibly have".

-Dale Carnegie

MICROCHAPTER 6: You are not alone.

This concept totally shifted my overall perspective of this disease. There is something to the feeling of connecting with others with type 1 diabetes that provides more benefit that I believe words can truly describe. It's the mutual respect, knowing that if others can do it, so can you... AND if you can do it, so can others. As humans we are designed to value community. It's an important part of survival so we are geared to subconsciously prioritize it. I truly believe that if you can take the isolation out of your life with diabetes, you can take a part of the burden out. There is an emotional discomfort that leaves when the isolation with diabetes leaves. Isolation, after all, is one of the worst forms of punishment in the US prison system.

Connection is a feeling. It can be cultivated through an in person hang out, a once a year conference, summer camp, a phone call, a text, reading an online blog forum, watching a YouTube video, etc. There are unlimited ways to connect with people with type 1 diabetes on the internet. Just like a prescription or an exercise program, timing and frequency can make a big difference.

You are already on your way to improving the diabetes connections in your life by doing this workbook. This program really was created to connect with you. It was designed with the collaboration of lessons from similar experiences, perspectives and emotions in mind. The other important connection that I hope you strengthen over the next 21 days is the connection with yourself.

In addition to connecting with yourself and with me through explained experiences, realize that you have already connected with the type 1 diabetes community in a big way. When you purchased this workbook, 20% of the proceeds will go to Texas Lions Camp, a free camp for kids with type 1 diabetes. Little humans, just like you pricking fingers and counting carbs. That is beautiful. You've given back in a big way. Please take a minute to let that sink in and give yourself some props for giving to the community.

When was the last time, if ever, that you spoke to someone else with type 1 diabetes?

- Do you have a friend with type one you haven't reached out to in while? Yes ○ /No ○
- Are you avoiding meeting people with type one for a reason? Yes ○ /No ○
- Are you putting yourself in the right environment to thrive? Yes ○ /No ○

This is a real thing. If you are doing this course you have access to the internet. There are countless blogs, Facebook groups, support chats out there. If you haven't reached out, I challenge you to dig deep and ask yourself **why**? Yep, that's right, you know the drill by now. Write it out.

Is this something you want to change? Yes ○ /No ○

If you don't know where to meet someone with type 1, check out these websites as a starting place.

- Google search; TuDiabetes, BeyondType1, JDRF conference in your area.
- Facebook search; groups for people with diabetes: T1D athletes, T1D moms, etc.
- Podcasts; Diabetics Doing Things by Rob Howe, T1D, Ask me about My Type 1 by Walt Drennan T1D

This is a list of people who are high-performers in their field who also happen to have type 1 diabetes. They have found roles to excel in while managing diabetes in their life. I find it incredibly inspiring. This list is in no way exhaustive.

Dexter Bean - Auto racing Driver

Bertrand Burgalat - Musician and Music producer

Carol Channing - Actress and Comedian

Damon Dash - Entrepreneur, co-founder of Roc-A-Fella Records and Rocawear

Buster Douglas - Professional Boxer

Carstan Fischer - Olympic Field Hockey Player

Devin Grayson - Writer of comic books and a Novelists

Jay Cutler - NFL Football Player Chicago Bears

Dr. Nicole Johnson - Miss America in 1999

Bret Micheals - Lead singer of the band Poison / The Celebrity Apprentice Winner

Nick Jonas - Singer, the band The Jonas Brothers

Theresa May - Prime Minister of the United Kingdom

Anne Rice - Novelest, most notable The Vampire Novel Series

Mary Tyler Moore - "The Mary Tyler Moore" show and Actress

Elliot Yamin - 3rd place finisher of American Idol, season 5

Sonia Sotomayor - Justice on the US Supreme Court

Gary Hall Jr. - Swimmer, 10 time gold-winning Olympic medalist

Crystal Bowersox - American Idol finalist in 2010

Jean Smart - Actress, first break in Designing Women

Dorian Gregory - Actor in Soul Train, Charmed, Baywatch Nights

Damon Dash jumped to fame as the former CEO and co-founder of Roc-A-Fella Records with Shawn "Jay-Z" Carter and Kareem "Biggs" Burke

Dr. Stephen Ponder - Diabetes Educator of the Year X2

Este Haim - Pop singer in the band Haim.

Eric Pasely - Country Singer

Jennifer Bartel's - Famous actress, "Shrill, American Women & Friends of people".

Mark Andrews - Baltimore Ravens Tight End

Taylor Luderman - Broadway Star

Ryan Reed - NASCAR Driver

Sam Talbot - Celebrity Chef, philanthropist, founder of Beyond Type 1

Dr. Nat Strand - Anesthesiologist and Amazing Race Competitor

Roddy Riddle - Ultramarathoner

Katelyn Prominski Baud - Professional Ballet Dancer

Brandon Green - Former NFL football player

Kendal Simmons - NFL football player

Jordan Morris - Professional Soccer Player

Victor Garber - Actor and Singer

Derek Theler - Actor in Desperate Housewives and Marvel's New Warriors.

Methias Steiner - Weightlifter and Olympic Gold Medalist

Adam Morrison - Basketball Player

Brandon Marrow - Major League Baseball Player.

Dr. Robert Lawrence - Founder of British Diabetic Association

MICROCHAPTER 7: Find the good.

I have met many people with type 1 diabetes who have used the disease in their favor. They have reflected and acknowledged the lessons type 1 has taught them and applied the teachings to other places in their lives. This habit is not only empowering, but it actually makes diabetes an overall good thing in the grand scheme of their life. It makes diabetes a teacher, a place for growth, a way to show love to themselves, a challenge to overcome. It makes diabetes a joy in a sense, if you want to take it that far.

I challenge you to do the same. Think of just one positive thing diabetes has taught you and write it out below. If nothing comes to mind immediately, check out the example below and keep brainstorming.

Example: When I started wearing an insulin pump. I had to learn to not let what other people think about my appearance bother me so much. It taught me to feel okay with standing out.

Now think of one way you can apply this lesson to a non-diabetes related thing in your life.

Example continued: When it came time to give a speech in English class, I wasn't as worried about standing out and talking in front of everyone.

Okay, great work. Now do this a few more times below to start showing yourself what an alternate or new or refreshed mindset about diabetes in your life can look like.

Diabetes lesson:

Applied life lesson:

Diabetes lesson:

Applied life lesson:

Diabetes lesson:

Applied life lesson:

Diabetes lesson:

Applied life lesson:

Diabetes lesson:

Applied life lesson:

A personal account: I know diabetes makes me a better doctor than I would have ever been without it. I actually accredit diabetes for inspiring me to go to medical school in the first place. Diabetes has contributed to making my life wonderful. It has allowed me to write this story, it has allowed me to write this story and use my life insight to give back in a fulfilling way. I like to think that is pretty beautiful. I am so very grateful for diabetes in my life.

MICROCHAPTER 8: Creating your new reality.

Your mindset. It's your mindset, you get to choose it. Not your parents, not your friends, and especially not your doctor. How you feel about diabetes is completely and ultimately up to you.

Take a second to skim through the responses you've written to all the questions in this workbook so far. You may be surprised by what you've written. It may feel great to get some things out, you may look back at them realizing you do or don't want these thought patterns.

Now choose. Choose how you want to feel about diabetes in your life. At this moment. This is your time. You've come this far. You are so capable. Decide and write it down.

Now answer the questions below from the perspective of **your chosen intentional mindset** above.

Diabetes is:

Diabetes makes me feel:

I am:

Summarize the above 4 responses into a single powerful impactful sentence. Try to make this sentence from a positive point of view, affirming what you want, not what you don't want. For example, "I am whole" instead of, " I am not broken". "I am my own hero" instead of "I am not a victim". "Diabetes can be an asset to my life because XYZ," instead of "Diabetes isn't that bad because XYZ."

Write it below:

This will provide some insight and be helpful on your first day of journaling below. Remember, it will be helpful to come back to this section when brainstorming for future questions on Day 1.

MICROCHAPTER 9: You are capable.

The implementation step. The bring-it-to-life step. The make a lasting impact step.

There was an incredible study done, where a group of people were asked to complete a gratitude list every morning for 21 days and their well-being was measured through a survey. ONE WHOLE YEAR later they took this survey and it turns out their measurements of wellbeing were higher than the control group in the study. That's a significant measure, 5 mins a day for 21 days, a total of ~ 2.5 hours of journaling things they were grateful for made them happier for a minimum of a year later.

There was a similar study specific to our lives that took two groups of people with type 1 diabetes and their caregivers. One group was asked to fill out forms for 8 weeks relating to positive psychology and gratitude. The other group received a form of diabetes education. Questionnaires were given to each group about quality of life and coping. The group with the positive psychology intervention had a statistically significant increase in quality of life, when compared to the education group, three months after completion of this 8 weeks study. This is a pretty profound example that shows the way we think about diabetes can impact the way we perceive the quality of our lives. It also shows that creating a habit of positive psychology and gratitude in our own lives is an intervention that may be worthwhile to learn. After all, that is probably part of the reason why you are doing this course in the first place, to improve your quality of life.

An important part of this study is that they repeated the quality of life questionnaire six months after completion of the 8-week intervention and there was no difference in responses from the group, meaning that the intervention doesn't make long term permanent change. My takeaway point from this is that if we choose to change our thought patterns, it takes a consistent habit to create lasting change.

This study has more detail and more to learn from it, here is the link for those interested.

Randomized Trial of a Positive Psychology Intervention for Adolescents With Type 1 Diabetes.

J Pediatr Psychol. 2019 Jun 1;44(5):620-629. doi: 10.1093/jpepsy/jsz006.

Jaser SS1, Whittemore R2, Choi L3, Nwosu S3, Russell WE1,3.

https://www.ncbi.nlm.nih.gov/pubmed/30840084

The biggest step of mindset change, in my opinion, is deciding which areas of your mindset you would like to expand. This for me has had a lasting impact, the decision and desire of this mindset change has stuck with me regardless of habit creation. It is the habit creation however, that has allowed me to attain it. The next part of this workbook will teach you how to create a habit of learning to change your thoughts and prime your mindset every morning for this desired change.

"You'll never change your life until you change something you do daily. The secret of your success is found in your daily routine". - John C. Maxwell

THE DAILY JOURNAL.

The daily journal that follows is designed to be done first thing in the morning. It takes 5 minutes or less and should be easy to squeeze into even the busiest of days.

Tips for helping yourself follow through include setting an alarm on your phone for some time within the hour of waking. Don't let yourself snooze the alarm or turn off the sound until you are looking at this journal. Put it on your bedside table, next to your blood glucose meter, by your toothbrush, on the coffee pot, by your keys, or somewhere it will be seen as you go through your already established morning routine. If you decide to complete it on your computer keep the tab open or save the file to your desktop.

The goal here is to reduce the activation energy of you getting to the journal. Once you're there it will be straightforward and quick to complete. If you miss a day don't beat yourself up, just do it later on, or the next day or skip it. The goal is not perfection, the goal is mindset progress. This should be an easy yet impactful process. Don't overthink it, just answer the questions, write your mantra, and start your day with an influenced perspective. You can't mess this up! I've got your back, I wrote you a daily letter to help keep you encouraged and accountable along this change.

Remember it's just 21 days and if the time commitment overwhelms you then commit to just starting tomorrow. After you complete it tomorrow, ask yourself if you think you can commit to one more day and continue from there. See where it takes you. If a 21-day goal seems impossible, just break it up into 21 small 1-day goals. You got this.

AFFIRMATIONS:

An important part of this daily journal will be affirmations, or what we can consider as daily reminders of our new mindset desires and goals. This will help keep us on track in the direction we want to move in. In order to do this, we need to establish affirmations that explain and remind of us of the new thoughts we chose.

You are already on a role! I recommend going ahead to the Day #1 journal below and creating your affirmations for the remainder of this mindset reset. Day 1 is designed to be a set up day, after you have answered these questions for the first time it will likely feel easier and more natural to answer the morning journal questions the following days.

WANT TO SHARE THE LOVE?

If you want to post your journal responses and you would like me to follow along use the hashtag #T1Dmindsetreset and tag me @drhannahhamlin. I'd love to see your growth over these next three weeks. Feel free to post your new insight, lightbulb moments, and share the positive quotes. Giving back and paying things forward often feels really good.

Join the exclusive Facebook group for people doing this workbook. You can search *Type 1 Diabetes Mindset Reset Team* or head to this link to get connected with other readers. https://www.facebook.com/groups/802497003673283/

DAY # 1:

How did you feel about diabetes being part of your day today? One being not so great, ten being the best you've ever felt. Try to make this an observation, not a judgement. Highlight a number: 1, 2, 3, 4, 5, 6, 7, 8, 9, 10.

Gratitude:

- List one thing you are grateful for that diabetes has taught you.
  I am grateful that diabetes has taught me...

List one thing you are grateful for that you accomplished or experienced since your diagnosis.
I am grateful for...

List one thing that you are grateful for in your life today that has nothing to do with diabetes.
I am grateful for...

Affirmation: Write out your new diabetes mantra and say it out loud. The more repetitions you have, the stronger you will make your neural pathways, the more likely it will manifest in your life. **Remember to refer to what you wrote in Chapter 8 for insight.**

Example: I have diabetes, I am not diabetes. I am ..... and capable of becoming a .... My thoughts impact my reality. I love me. I love my life. I love the way things are progressing.

Here are some more suggestions to assist in creating your own positive affirmations. The chapter titles of this workbook are designed to serve as suggestions and reminders of things you learned from each section. Feel free to use the chapters that affected you emotionally the most or use them all.

1 I am not diabetes.
2 I am not broken.
3 My thoughts about diabetes impact my actions.
4 It's not my fault.
5 I choose to be a hero.
6 I am not alone.
7 I choose to see the good.
8 I choose to create a new reality.
9 I am capable.

Here are some more examples that may feel better to you:

I am human. -> input your name or favorite role.

I am whole. -> badass, incredible, amazing, perfect just the way I am.

I believe that my thoughts will control my actions and luckily I get to choose my thoughts.

I am at ease. I am worthy. I am enough.

I choose to be my own hero. I chose to think great things about myself.

I am connected. I enjoy my community.

I choose love. I choose to be optimistic.

I am creating my dream life. I have a great relationship with diabetes.

I got this. I can do this. I am doing this.

Actionable steps & Intention: Write out one intention as an actionable step today. These small intentions are here to help you start building and incorporating tools for mindset in your mental health toolbox. It's okay if they don't happen everyday. The idea is to create positive intentions and each day so that your mind can start to recognize areas in your life that you have opportunities to use these new patterns. Don't be hard on yourself here. Just pick a positive tool you want to work on and write it out. Let the rest be easy.

Examples: I am open to/would love to/will...

...reach out to an old friend with type 1 diabetes that I haven't seen in a while.

...listen to a diabetes podcast.

...call a close friend/family member if I have a rough diabetes moment.

...remind myself not to let an out of range blood sugar number make me feel bad about my ability to take care of myself.

...remind myself I'm strong if I have a low and want to eat more carbs than I really need to treat it.

...act optimistic about my diabetes tech if someone asks me about it.

...test my blood sugar in front of others and be proud of all sides of me.

"Happiness is a habit—cultivate it".

-Elbert Hubbard

DAY # 2:

Good morning,

Just a reminder from a fellow friend with type 1 diabetes that you are not alone. There are lots of people out there testing their blood sugar and taking insulin today. You are so capable of making this life as happy and healthy as you want to make it.

Give yourself props for starting something new today. I hope you are able to realize your progress and feel accomplished!

Cheers, Dr. Hannah

Gratitude:

- List one thing you are grateful for that diabetes has taught you.
  I am grateful for

  List one thing you are grateful for that you accomplished or experienced since your diagnosis.
  I am grateful for

  List one thing that you are grateful for in your life today that has nothing to do with diabetes.
  I am grateful for

Affirm: Write out your new diabetes mantra and say it out loud.

Intention: Set one simple positive intention for the day:

"Motivation is what gets you started. Habit is what keeps you going".

- Jim Rohn

DAY # 3:

Hey There,

The first few days of creating a new routine will be the hardest. Fine tuning the flow of adding one more thing to your morning schedule will get easier. As you create new thought processes, you will likely get more efficient at answering the questions. Stick with it this week and keep an eye out for results and positive changes in the way you see things throughout the day.

Thanks, Dr. Hannah

Gratitude:

- List one thing you are grateful for that diabetes has taught you.
  I am grateful for

  List one thing you are grateful for that you accomplished or experienced since your diagnosis.
  I am grateful for

  List one thing that you are grateful for in your life today that has nothing to do with diabetes.
  I am grateful for

Affirm: Write out your new diabetes mantra and say it out loud.

Intention: Set one simple positive intention for the day:

"With everything that has happened to you, you can either feel sorry for yourself or treat what has happened as a gift. Everything is either an opportunity to grow or an obstacle to keep you from growing. You get to choose." - Wayne Dyer

DAY # 4:

Hi Friend,

You are stronger than you think and capable of more than you know. Do you know that it is possible for people with type 1 diabetes to have blood glucose levels like those of adults without diabetes? You may not have been told this before. I know I found out after many many years of being type 1. There are people with type 1 diabetes that have HbA1c levels in the 4-5%'s. It takes knowledge and diligence but there are some people out there making it happen. Kudos to them! It may not be what all of us desire for our level of control, but if it is something you want or strive for, it is totally possible.

Thanks, Dr. Hannah

Gratitude:

- List one thing you are grateful for that diabetes has taught you.
  I am grateful for

  List one thing you are grateful for that you accomplished or experienced since your diagnosis.
  I am grateful for

  List one thing that you are grateful for in your life today that has nothing to do with diabetes.
  I am grateful for

Affirm: Write out your new diabetes mantra and say it out loud.

Intention: Set one simple positive intention for the day:

"You'll never change your life until you change something you do daily. The secret of your success is found in your daily routine".

-John C. Maxwell

DAY # 5:

Hey There,

Remember that it's not about being perfect. If you skip a day, that's okay, you can pick back up the next morning. If you have to take a few days off, that's okay too. This course is to help you work through your thoughts around diabetes in your own time. It's here to serve you, not judge you or expect you to be perfect. This is about learning to love yourself and your life the way it is. If you miss a day, love your way through it. Motivate yourself to take the next best step for you.

Peace, Dr. Hannah

Gratitude:

- List one thing you are grateful for that diabetes has taught you.
  I am grateful for

  List one thing you are grateful for that you accomplished or experienced since your diagnosis.
  I am grateful for

  List one thing that you are grateful for in your life today that has nothing to do with diabetes.
  I am grateful for

Affirm: Write out your new diabetes mantra and say it out loud.

Intention: Set one simple positive intention for the day:

"May your choices reflect your hopes not your fears."

- **Nelson Mandela**

DAY # 6:

Dear Improving One,

You and your blood sugars are separate entities. You CAN have high blood sugar and keep your mindset positive. You CAN have a low and still have a great day. It's not always easy and it's okay if it doesn't happen that way. It's important to remind ourselves that it IS possible to control our emotions regardless of our blood sugar levels. We don't have to let blood sugar levels that we don't like make us not like ourselves in that moment. We are so intertwined with our blood sugar levels physically, they can affect our energy levels, thirst, and muscular strength. They don't have to affect our thoughts though, they don't have to change the way we talk to ourselves or the emotions we feel.

You are making progress. Believe this.

Thanks, Dr. Hannah

Gratitude:

- List one thing you are grateful for that diabetes has taught you.
  I am grateful for

  List one thing you are grateful for that you accomplished or experienced since your diagnosis.
  I am grateful for

  List one thing that you are grateful for in your life today that has nothing to do with diabetes.
  I am grateful for

Affirm: Write out your new diabetes mantra and say it out loud.

Intention: Set one simple positive intention for the day:

"Life is 10% what happens to me and 90% of how I react to it".
- John C. Maxwell

DAY # 7:

Hello Gorgeous People,

Here is some personal insight.

You would think, in fact I did, that diabetes teaches us only independence. We have life threatening responsibilities daily and we have to learn to stand up for ourselves in situations. We find ourselves telling others that, in fact we did not get diabetes from eating too much candy. We sit on the kitchen floor alone, at 3am, drinking out of a juice box to treat a terrifying blood sugar in the 30's. We know independence already by default, a noble yet humbling version of it. We dose our own life saving drug with life altering side effects every single day. We are really independent. What I also know is that I'd prefer not to do it alone.

What diabetes has taught me though, is that I wouldn't be doing as well as I am if I didn't have someone to text at 3am from the kitchen floor or a friend to laugh with about the ridiculous misconceptions of diabetes. Diabetes is better with other people, just like life is better with other people. I've learned that independence is a given and that letting other people in has been my challenge. With the support of my family, friends, and others with type 1 diabetes, diabetes is more doable in the long term.

Ask yourself today, how many people do you know with type 1 diabetes? Can you think of a connection you have with someone where you would feel comfortable reaching out to them with a question? If not, are you ready to reach out for some comradery online? If this is a deficiency in your life and you haven't already, I recommend you check out some of the resources listed in chapter 6.

You may have a few friends with type 1 diabetes and be totally content with that. Consider touching base with them today? Asking them how their life with diabetes is going.

Thanks, Dr. Hamlin

Gratitude: List one thing you are grateful for that diabetes has taught you.
I am grateful for

- List one thing you are grateful for that you accomplished or experienced since your diagnosis.
  I am grateful for

  List one thing that you are grateful for in your life today that has nothing to do with diabetes.
  I am grateful for

Affirm: Write out your new diabetes mantra and say it out loud.

Intention: Set one simple positive intention for the day:

We are what we repeatedly do. Excellence, then, is not an act but a habit.

- Will Durant based on Aristotle's teachings

DAY # 8:

Dear Human,

It's okay if it hurts. It's hard work sometimes. It's okay to cry if you need to.

Tearing yourself down or your disease down with your words is not likely to help you in the long run. There are other ways to get relief from negative emotions. From my experience, it's been about letting the light in and giving less attention to the darkness. This doesn't mean being unaware of what the darkness or complications or side effects of our decisions are. This just means putting most of our attention towards the good. Hopefully by now you know your good. You are starting to practice bringing the good to your conscious mind every morning.

Thanks, Dr. Hannah

Gratitude:

- List one thing you are grateful for that diabetes has taught you.
  I am grateful for

  List one thing you are grateful for that you accomplished or experienced since your diagnosis.
  I am grateful for

  List one thing that you are grateful for in your life today that has nothing to do with diabetes.
  I am grateful for

Affirm: Write out your new diabetes mantra and say it out loud.

Intention: Set one simple positive intention for the day:

"In essence, if we want to direct our lives, we must take control of our consistent actions. It's not what we do once in a while that shapes our lives, but what we do consistently". - Tony Robbins

DAY # 9:

Hey You,

Subtle reminder; You are not broken. I used to feel like a human with a part missing who was constantly spending hours a day trying to make up for what my body couldn't do anymore. That sucked. It took A LOT of self-reflection and a little bit of maturity to finally come to terms with the fact that I am a whole, perfectly functioning, deserving, and loving human being. Diabetes has taught me that what makes you a whole person isn't your functional beta cell count or anything physical for that matter, it's about who you are and who you think you are.

Have a great day, Hannah

Gratitude:

- List one thing you are grateful for that diabetes has taught you.
  I am grateful for

  List one thing you are grateful for that you accomplished or experienced since your diagnosis.
  I am grateful for

  List one thing that you are grateful for in your life today that has nothing to do with diabetes.
  I am grateful for

Affirm: Write out your new diabetes mantra and say it out loud.

Intention: Set one simple positive intention for the day:

"You have power over your mind – not outside events. Realize this, and you will find strength". - Marcus Aurelius

DAY # 10:

Hey There,

Today I'd love to share with you some of my personal insight.

That 'up arrow' feeling. The feeling you get when you know your blood sugar is spiking up in a direction you don't want it to be because of a decision you know you could have made differently. It's rough. For me it use to represent the feeling of immediate regret, of self-shaming for not being 'better' or more intentional about my last minute decisions. I'm looking at it now, a blood sugar of 240 up arrow on my dexcom (continuous glucose monitor) because I chose to eat a bowl of blueberries immediately when I got home instead of the healthy balanced meal that could have been bolused for ahead of time. I did it to me. I was stressed and hungry and craving something sweet. I did it to satisfy my immediate craving and bolused after basically predicting this would happen. Why did I do this? Why would I intentionally do this to myself when I know good glucose control is high on my priorities list? There are a lot of potential reasons, but I think the reason lies mostly in the fact that I was far out of a state of comfort. I was stressed, I didn't feel well, I was in a fight or flight mode. My sympathetic nervous system was driving and all I cared about was fixing my current physical & emotional state. When we are in a state of urgency or emergency our brain kicks into 'stabilize' mode where we aren't thinking ahead about our long-term goals, we are thinking about how to make ourselves feel more 'safe' right now. You may be familiar with this concept in your own life when it comes to over treating lows.

What can we learn from this? That stress management is important to our health, to the likelihood of accomplishing our future long-term goals and to how we feel in the moment. Notice that it wasn't my diabetes fault that I let myself get stressed on my way home from work. It wasn't diabete's fault that I didn't take insulin until after I ate my snack. It wasn't diabete's fault that my brain was in 'stabilize now' mode. It was however, diabetes fault that I was reminded of this important lesson. Stress matters. Thanks diabetes.

Dr. Hannah

Gratitude:

- List one thing you are grateful for that diabetes has taught you.
  I am grateful for

List one thing you are grateful for that you accomplished or experienced since your diagnosis.
I am grateful for

List one thing that you are grateful for in your life today that has nothing to do with diabetes.
I am grateful for

Affirm: Write out your new diabetes mantra and say it out loud.

Intention: Set one simple positive intention for the day:

"When you have exhausted all possibilities, remember this: you haven't".

- Thomas A. Edison

DAY # 11:

Hello People,

Today is a great day.

Also, you should be so freaking proud of yourself today because you've completed more than half of a project you set out to do. You are a go getter. You are making a positive change in your life. You are rocking it!

Take some time today to treat yourself. You deserve it.

Thanks, Dr. Hannah

Gratitude:

- List one thing you are grateful for that diabetes has taught you.
  I am grateful for

  List one thing you are grateful for that you accomplished or experienced since your diagnosis.
  I am grateful for

  List one thing that you are grateful for in your life today that has nothing to do with diabetes.
  I am grateful for

Affirm: Write out your new diabetes mantra and say it out loud.

Intention: Set one simple positive intention for the day:

"Freedom is being who you are unapologetically". - Dr. Robin Smith

DAY # 12:

Hi Beautiful Humans,

You're halfway through this challenge. If you haven't completed each day until now, don't judge yourself. This is a process, you don't have to fill it out perfectly in order for it to work. Trust the process, trust yourself to shift the perspectives that you came here to change.

Take 30 seconds to think back to the day you signed up for this course. Think about how you felt, what your reason 'why' was, what you wanted to change in your life. Let that sink in a bit.

Reflecting can help re-cultivate motivation. Connecting with your 'why' is always a good thing.

Thanks, Dr. Hannah

Gratitude:

- List one thing you are grateful for that diabetes has taught you.
  I am grateful for

  List one thing you are grateful for that you accomplished or experienced since your diagnosis.
  I am grateful for

  List one thing that you are grateful for in your life today that has nothing to do with diabetes.
  I am grateful for

Affirm: Write out your new diabetes mantra and say it out loud.

Intention: Set one simple positive intention for the day:

"The world as we have created it is a process of our thinking. It cannot be changed without changing our thinking". -Albert Einstein

DAY # 13:

Good Morning, it's going to be a great day!

Love. Self-love helps most things in life. Think of 3 things you love about yourself today. Repeat them three times.

"**Self**-approval and **self**-acceptance in the now are the main keys to positive changes in every area of our lives." - Louise Hay

That is all.

- Dr. Han

Gratitude:

- List one thing you are grateful for that diabetes has taught you.
  I am grateful for

  List one thing you are grateful for that you accomplished or experienced since your diagnosis.
  I am grateful for

  List one thing that you are grateful for in your life today that has nothing to do with diabetes.
  I am grateful for

Affirm: Write out your new diabetes mantra and say it out loud.

Intention: Set one simple positive intention for the day:

“No one saves us but ourselves. No one can and no one may.

We ourselves must walk the path”. - Buddha

DAY # 14:
Pay it forward.

Hello hello,

Talking about diabetes with others has its challenges. Having to guess how much medical background the person has, fearing any stigma, not wanting to have the same conversation with others over and over about the sticker on the back of your arm. It's not easy, but sometimes it can be worth it. This week, if diabetes comes up with someone outside of your household, try spinning the description in a positive direction. Make note of how it makes you feel. For me this exercise can be empowering.

With love, Dr. Hannah

Gratitude:

- List one thing you are grateful for that diabetes has taught you.
  I am grateful for

  List one thing you are grateful for that you accomplished or experienced since your diagnosis.
  I am grateful for

  List one thing that you are grateful for in your life today that has nothing to do with diabetes.
  I am grateful for

Affirm: Write out your new diabetes mantra and say it out loud.

Intention: Set one simple positive intention for the day:

"And once you understand that habits can change, you have the freedom and the responsibility to remake them". -Charles Duhigg

DAY # 15:
It's okay if you feel like you're faking it.

Hey there,

It's okay to cry. It's no secret that diabetes makes me cry all the time. I used to feel guilty about it, like I was weak and not strong enough to handle what the world had given me. Now, I realize that crying is a sign giving my emotions some recognition. I see importance in taking time to acknowledge when diabetes overwhelms me. No matter what causes the tears, reflection in that moment seems to be a positive thing in the long run.

Your T1D Friend.

Gratitude:

- List one thing you are grateful for that diabetes has taught you.
  I am grateful for

  List one thing you are grateful for that you accomplished or experienced since your diagnosis.
  I am grateful for

  List one thing that you are grateful for in your life today that has nothing to do with diabetes.
  I am grateful for

Affirm: Write out your new diabetes mantra and say it out loud.

Intention: Set one simple positive intention for the day:

"We do not have to become heroes overnight. Just a step at a time, meeting each thing that comes up, seeing it is not as dreadful as it appeared, discovering we have the strength to stare it down". - Eleanor Roosevelt

DAY # 16:
5 daily reminders for yourself.

Hello Gorgeous Humans,

Here are 5 reminders for you to tell yourself.

1 I am amazing
2 I can do anything
3 Positivity is a choice
4 I celebrate my individuality
5 I am prepared to succeed

That is all.

Make it a good one,

Dr. Han

Gratitude:

- List one thing you are grateful for that diabetes has taught you.
  I am grateful for

  List one thing you are grateful for that you accomplished or experienced since your diagnosis.
  I am grateful for

  List one thing that you are grateful for in your life today that has nothing to do with diabetes.
  I am grateful for

Affirm: Write out your new diabetes mantra and say it out loud.

Intention: Set one simple positive intention for the day:

“Let today be the day you give up who you've been for who you can become”.

-Hal Elrod

DAY # 17:

Dear Fellow T1D,

You are so strong. You are capable. You are making a positive change in your life. Diabetes is a challenge and you rise to the challenge every day. This should be pretty empowering. Remind yourself, you are showing up and not giving up every day. That's admirable.

Happy day,

Dr. Hannah

Gratitude:

- List one thing you are grateful for that diabetes has taught you.
  I am grateful for

  List one thing you are grateful for that you accomplished or experienced since your diagnosis.
  I am grateful for

  List one thing that you are grateful for in your life today that has nothing to do with diabetes.
  I am grateful for

Affirm: Write out your new diabetes mantra and say it out loud.

Intention: Set one simple positive intention for the day:

"Strength does not come from winning. Your struggles develop your strengths". -Arnold Schwarzenegger

DAY # 18:

You are enough.

Hello Guys,

Today, I want to remind you that you are enough. No matter what you're growing through right now, no matter how hard it is or how impossible a resolution may seem, you are enough and you are capable of making your dreams come true.

Peace.

Gratitude:

- List one thing you are grateful for that diabetes has taught you.
  I am grateful for

  List one thing you are grateful for that you accomplished or experienced since your diagnosis.
  I am grateful for

  List one thing that you are grateful for in your life today that has nothing to do with diabetes.
  I am grateful for

Affirm: Write out your new diabetes mantra and say it out loud.

Intention: Set one simple positive intention for the day:

"Success is the sum of small efforts repeated day in and day out".

-Robert Collier

DAY # 19:

Good Morning Sunshine,

The world is full of beautiful things, it's time to start realizing that you are one of them. It's important for people to know that contrary to popular belief, it is absolutely possible to live a life with diabetes that is healthy and happy, no beta cells needed.

With love, Dr. Hannah

Gratitude:

- List one thing you are grateful for that diabetes has taught you.
  I am grateful for

  List one thing you are grateful for that you accomplished or experienced since your diagnosis.
  I am grateful for

  List one thing that you are grateful for in your life today that has nothing to do with diabetes.
  I am grateful for

Affirm: Write out your new diabetes mantra and say it out loud.

Intention: Set one simple positive intention for the day:

“Practice isn't the thing you do once you're good.

It's the thing you do that makes you good”.

-Malcolm Gladwell

DAY # 20:
What's next?

Hey,

What's next on your journey through life with type 1 diabetes? You may have identified places in your life where you want to continue growing. You may have set goals. You may have taken this course for what it is and you are ready to move back to your non-journaling mornings. All things are good. I challenge you to do what feels right. By completing this course in full or in part, you have taken a step in elevating your emotions, perspectives, and mindset.

Be proud my friend, be proud.

Looking for a next step? Here are three Mindset books that drastically helped me on my journey to an intentional frame of mind.

- The Power of Now - Eckhart Tole
  - Teaches about living in the moment and provides ways and insight to quit continuous thinking in your mind.
- Loving What Is - Bryan Tracy
  - Provides insight on working through challenging times in life and how to find happiness by working through your thoughts.
- Sugar Surfing - Dr. Stephen Ponder
  - The number one book I recommend to people with type 1 diabetes. Dr. Ponder has type 1 diabetes himself. He works as a Pediatric Endocrinologist, is the medical director of Texas Lions Camp (the camp for kids with type 1 diabetes that you helped donate to when buying this course) and is an international speaker. The first chapter of his book has an incredibly well written perspective on diabetes from his life and his extensive experiences of helping others with type 1 diabetes.

Gratitude:

- List one thing you are grateful for that diabetes has taught you.

I am grateful for

List one thing you are grateful for that you accomplished or experienced since your diagnosis.

I am grateful for

List one thing that you are grateful for in your life today that has nothing to do with diabetes.

I am grateful for

Affirm: Write out your new diabetes mantra and say it out loud.

Intention: Set one simple positive intention for the day:

"Want more confidence? Love yourself. Ready to finally set boundaries? Love yourself. Time to go after that dream? Love yourself. Ready to release your emotion? Love yourself. Your relationship with yourself, sets the tone for your entire life". - Thibaut

DAY # 21: Congratulations!

You are your own hero! You are an incredibly successful person who has faced challenges with your body that most people can't even imagine. You have experienced the monotony and the constant roller coaster of having type 1 diabetes, and through all of that you have completed a challenging task towards elevating your life. You are on the right track to great things. You have taken a step towards achieving your goals. You are not alone. You can rely on yourself. You are whole. You are capable of making your wildest dreams come true. You are you, and no one else gets to be, so I challenge you from here to make the best of it.

Keep practicing unconditional self-love. Keep learning about how best to take care of your body. Keep progressing in life with an intentional mindset and know that you have the power, at any time, to control your thoughts. You are limitless and type 1 diabetes has given you the opportunity to learn incredibly positive lessons in this life. You are your own hero.

I'm so proud of you.

And guys... thanks for participating in this course, it was a longtime dream of mine. Thank you for the fulfillment and joy I have received from the privilege of letting me give back and thank you for reminding me that I am not alone.

If this course touched you, changed you, helped you, brought anything positive to your life I ask that you share your story, pass on the positivity. I'd love to hear what you've learned.

Let's stay in touch.

With all of my heart, Dr. Hamlin

- How positive did you feel about diabetes being part of your day today?
  - Circle a number: 1 2 3 4 5 6 7 8 9 10
  - Take this time to go back and see if your numbers have changed since day 1.

Gratitude:

- List one thing you are grateful for that diabetes has taught you.
  I am grateful for

List one thing you are grateful for that you accomplished or experienced since your diagnosis.
I am grateful for

List one thing that you are grateful for in your life today that has nothing to do with diabetes.
I am grateful for

Affirm: Write out your new diabetes mantra and say it out loud.

Intention: Set one simple positive intention for the day:

"Love yourself first and everything else falls into line. You really have to love yourself to get anything done in this world."

– Lucille Ball

"Your life is as good as your mindset." - Unknown

Disclaimer: This book details the author's personal experiences with and opinions about type 1 diabetes and mindset. The author is not your healthcare provider. The author and publisher are providing this book and its contents on an "as is" basis and make no representations or warranties of any kind with respect to this book or its contents. The author disclaims all such representations and warranties, including for example warranties of merchantability and healthcare for a particular purpose. In addition, the author and publisher do not represent or warrant that the information accessible via this book is accurate, complete or current. The statements made about products and services have not been evaluated by the U.S. Food and Drug Administration. They are not intended to diagnose, treat, cure, or prevent any condition or disease. **Please consult with your own physician or healthcare specialist regarding the suggestions and recommendations made in this book.** Except as specifically stated in this book, neither the author or publisher, nor any authors, contributors, or other representatives will be liable for damages arising out of or in connection with the use of this book. This is a comprehensive limitation of liability that applies to all damages of any kind, including (without limitation) compensatory; direct, indirect or consequential damages; loss of data, income or profit; loss of or damage to property and claims of third parties. **You understand that this book is not intended as a substitute for consultation with a licensed healthcare practitioner, such as your physician**. Before you begin any healthcare program, or change your lifestyle in any way, you will consult your physician or another licensed healthcare practitioner to ensure that you are in good health and that the examples contained in this book will not harm you. This book provides content related to physical and/or mental health issues. As such, use of this book implies your acceptance of this disclaimer. The Content is not intended to be a substitute for professional medical advice, diagnosis, or treatment. Always seek the advice of your **physician** or other qualified health provider with any questions you may have regarding a medical condition. If you are or become suicidal or homicidal, please contact your local **emergency medical services**.

www.ingramcontent.com/pod-product-compliance
Ingram Content Group UK Ltd.
Pitfield, Milton Keynes, MK11 3LW, UK
UKHW061829190726
13853UKWH00009B/2508